# CITIES

## PAST AND PRESENT

**Thunder Bay Press**
An imprint of Printers Row Publishing Group
9717 Pacific Heights Blvd, San Diego, CA 92121
www.thunderbaybooks.com • mail@thunderbaybooks.com

Printers Row Publishing Group is a division of Readerlink Distribution Services, LLC.

Thunder Bay Press is a registered trademark of Readerlink Distribution Services, LLC.

Correspondence regarding the content of this book should be sent to Thunder Bay Press, Editorial Department, at the above address. All other inquiries should be addressed to The Bright Press at the address below.

**Thunder Bay Press**
Publisher: Peter Norton
Associate Publisher: Ana Parker
Editor: Dan Mansfield

This book was conceived, designed, and produced by The Bright Press, an imprint of the Quarto Group, 1 Triptych Place, London SE1 9SH, United Kingdom.
www.quarto.com

**The Bright Press**
Publisher: James Evans
Editorial Director: Isheeta Mustafi
Art Director: James Lawrence
Managing Editor: Jacqui Sayers
Senior Editor: Dee Costello
Project Editor: Anna Southgate
Senior Designer: Emily Nazer
Design: JC Lanaway
Picture Research: Charlotte Rivers and Jane Lanaway
Text: Charlotte Rivers

Library of Congress Cataloging-in-Publication data available on request.

ISBN: 978-1-6672-0516-8

Printed in Malaysia

27 26 25 24 23    1 2 3 4 5

# CITIES

## PAST AND PRESENT

THUNDER BAY
P·R·E·S·S
San Diego, California

# CONTENTS

# INTRODUCTION

**PAST AND PRESENT** Taking you on a fascinating journey through time, *Cities Past and Present* explores the history and evolution of twenty-five of the world's most dynamic cities.

Every city has a story to tell. Often, it is one that can be revealed through the buildings and landmarks that define that city, from the pyramids of ancient Egypt in Cairo to the bullet-scarred streets of Berlin to engineering marvels such as San Francisco's Golden Gate Bridge. Using archival and present-day photographs, this book delves into the rich history of these twenty-five cities. Discover how New York's Times Square developed from a center for the horse-and-carriage industry to become one of the busiest theater and entertainment districts in the world. Learn about the fascinating transformation of Vancouver's downtown waterfront area. And witness the rapid growth and ever-changing skyline of the desert city of Dubai. Featuring photographs of the cities, past and present, side by side, there is no better way to see how they have changed over time.

▶ Past and present photographs allow you to examine a city's changing landscape more closely. Here, Berlin Cathedral is seen damaged during World War II and subsequently restored to its former glory.

The historic photographs in this book are genuine and the imperfections of their age only add to the richness of the stories they tell.

# LOS ANGELES

Home to the U.S. film industry, Los Angeles, in the heart of Southern California, is a sprawling metropolis surrounded by the Pacific Coast, the Santa Monica Mountains, and the San Fernando Valley. Originally settled by the Tongva and Chumash people, it was first colonized by the Spanish, before going under Mexican rule, and then eventually becoming part of the United States in 1847. Today, Los Angeles, or the City of Angels as it is affectionately known, is a culturally diverse city

often said to be the creative capital of the world. From film and television, to museums and galleries, to the music industry and surf beaches, L.A. has it all. Unlike many other U.S. cities, Los Angeles was not built on a grid system, but instead exists as individual suburbs connected by a network of freeways that give it a unique feel with stunning vistas of the surrounding mountains as you travel around the city.

◄ Los Angeles, 1927. On the horizon, you can just about make out the outline of Los Angeles City Hall. Completed in 1928 and standing at 452 feet tall, it was the city's tallest building for four decades.

▼ The city's skyline as it is today, complete with its famous smog. The three tallest buildings are the Wilshire Grand Center, the U.S. Bank Tower, and the Aon Center.

**HOLLYWOODLAND** Better known as Hollywood, Hollywoodland is synonymous with the U.S. movie and television industry. Often referred to as Tinseltown, the area is home to the country's leading film studios, as well as the Hollywood Walk of Fame and the iconic Hollywood sign. The sign sits in what was once rural and sparsely populated land before it was developed into the residential area of "Hollywoodland" in the early 1920s.

▲ Sitting high in the Hollywood Hills, the original Hollywoodland sign was part of a 1923 advertising campaign for a housing development that was billed as giving buyers "the luxury of metropolitan living with the glorious freedom of the hills."

▶ Today the shortened version is one of the best-known landmarks in the United States. The letters spelling "land" were removed in 1949, and the entire sign was replaced with a more durable steel structure in 1979.

**VINE STREET** Running between Hollywood's Franklin and Melrose Avenues, the intersection of Vine Street and Hollywood Boulevard has long been known for its association with the entertainment industry. It is home to three blocks of the Hollywood Walk of Fame and the Beaux Arts–style Broadway Hollywood Building, built in 1928 and named for the Broadway department store chain that occupied the building from 1931 to 1982. The most famous building here is the Capitol Records Building, which first opened in 1956.

▲ The Capitol Records Building, pictured here in the 1970s, sits on the corner of Hollywood Boulevard and Vine Street. The Broadway Hollywood Building can be seen in the distance to the right of the image.

▲ Sunset over Hollywood Boulevard and
Vine Street in more recent years, with
the distinctive circular design of the
Capitol Records Building—once dubbed
"a monstrous stack of records" by the
press—still taking center stage.

**GRIFFITH OBSERVATORY** Located in Griffith Park on Mount Hollywood and attracting 1.6 million visitors a year, the Griffith Observatory is the most visited public observatory in the world. It is also one of only a few producing live planetarium shows. First opening its doors on May 14, 1935, it sits high in the hills and has views of downtown Los Angeles, Hollywood, and the Pacific Ocean.

▲ Top: Griffith Observatory, ca. 1935. Originally built in the 1930s, the observatory underwent a major four-year renovation in the early 2000s. It remains a leader in astronomy.

▶ The observatory today, showing the Los Angeles skyline in the distance, now populated with numerous skyscrapers.

# SAN FRANCISCO

Widely regarded as the cultural center of Northern California, San Francisco, aka the Golden City, is known for its diverse architecture, hilly landscape, liberal community, and thriving music and arts scene. Originally the land of the Ohlone people, it was later colonized and went on to become the center of the California gold rush in the mid-1800s. It was later devastated by the 1906 earthquake and subsequent fires, which destroyed an estimated 80 percent of the city.

Numerous streets of stores and residential housing were lost in the earthquake and several landmark buildings collapsed, including City Hall, the Palace Hotel, the Chronicle Building, and St. Ignatius Church. Despite the widespread devastation, it did not take long for the city to begin to rebuild. The late twentieth century saw the dot-com era once again put San Francisco on the map and the city continues to thrive today as one of the biggest tech centers in the United States.

◄ **Market Street, 1906.** The view down Market Street, still smoldering in the aftermath of the earthquake and the ensuing three-day fire that consumed much of the city.

▼ First built in 1847, Market Street remains a major artery in the city. In 2020, a two-mile stretch of the road, from the ferry terminal to 10th Street, became car-free in a bid to make it safer for the tens of thousands of people who use it daily.

## SAN FRANCISCO EARTHQUAKE At 5:12 a.m.

on April 18, 1906, the city of San Francisco was rocked by a 7.9 magnitude earthquake that, to this day, remains one of the most significant earthquakes of all time. The quake lasted less than one minute but caused untold damage, as did the fires sparked by the event.

▶ Top: San Francisco's Market Street, on which many buildings were destroyed by the earthquake and subsequent fires, 1906. Bottom: The same view of Market Street just over 100 years later.

▶▶ Top: San Francisco's old city hall was completed in 1899, less than a decade before the earthquake damaged it beyond repair. Bottom: The new city hall, which encompasses two whole city blocks, was built in the Neoclassical style. It took two years to complete, opening in 1915.

**GOLDEN GATE BRIDGE** The Golden Gate Bridge sits over the Golden Gate, a mile-wide strait that connects San Francisco Bay to the Pacific Ocean. The bridge links San Francisco to Marin County to the north of the city. Its vibrant orange color—actually called International Orange—was chosen so that the bridge would blend into the surrounding scenery while being visible to ships in the fog.

◀ Top: Work on the bridge started with its two concrete piers and the towers. The cables were drawn between them, before the sections of roadway were lifted into position. Bottom: Construction of the bridge took four years, from early 1933 to mid-1937. It was a challenging build due to the strait's strong tides, heavy winds, frequent fogs, and thick salt air.

▲ The Golden Gate Bridge today. There is always at least one area of the bridge being painted at any given time. This is part of a regular maintenance program that helps protect the bridge's steel from rusting in the salty air.

**UNION SQUARE** This public plaza sits in downtown San Francisco surrounded by shops, restaurants, bars, and art galleries. It takes its name from the pro-Union rallies that were held in the square on the eve of the American Civil War. A historical marker in the square is inscribed with events that have taken place here, including the naming of the site as Union Square (1861–65), the introduction of the first cable cars (1877–88), and the dedication of the Dewey Memorial at its heart (1903).

▼ Union Square, early 1900s. Originally a huge sand dune, the area was transformed into a public park in 1850, under the leadership of San Francisco's first American mayor, John Geary.

▶ Today, Union Square remains a hub for public gatherings. While newer buildings surround the square, the Dewey Memorial at its center remains the same. It was dedicated to Admiral George Dewey by President Theodore Roosevelt.

**BAY BRIDGE** The San Francisco–Oakland Bay Bridge is a complex crossing that runs between the cities of San Francisco to the west and Oakland to the east, via Yerba Buena Island in the middle of San Francisco Bay. Designed by Charles H. Purcell, it opened in 1936, just six months before the Golden Gate Bridge.

▲ Construction of the bridge began in July 1933 and proved challenging for workers due to the depth of the bay. However, it took just three years to complete.

▶ The crossing to the west consists of two end-to-end suspension bridges. The eastern section was originally a cantilever structure but today is a self-anchored suspension bridge leading to a long, inclined viaduct.

# SEATTLE

Sitting between Puget Sound and Lake Washington in the Pacific Northwest, the waterfront city of Seattle is surrounded by ocean, rivers, forests, and lakes. Prior to European settlement in the late 1800s, the area had been home to the Duwamish people for thousands of years. The hilly city has seen many industrial booms (and busts) over the years, from

logging, shipping, and the late nineteenth-century gold rush, and is now home to some of the biggest players in both the shipping and aviation industries. In recent years this diverse and thriving city has become a magnet for companies in the software and technology industries and today it rivals San Francisco as the tech epicenter of the United States.

◀ **Aerial view of Seattle and the Space Needle, 1962. The Space Needle was built for the Century 21 Exposition, also known as Seattle's World Fair, held that year. The fair's theme was "The Age of Space," hence its futuristic design.**

▼ **The Space Needle stands at 605 feet tall and gives visitors 360-degree views of the city from a number of observation decks located within the saucer-shaped "top house." Visitors can reach the tower's top level by elevator, a journey that takes just 43 seconds.**

**DOWNTOWN WATERFRONT** Seattle's waterfront was once home to the Coast Salish people, who used the area to fish and hunt. However, after European settlement in the late 1700s, a number of wharves were built and it quickly became home to the city's maritime industry.

▲ Seattle's downtown waterfront, 1952, when it was still the center of the city's maritime industry. Running from left to right across the image is the Alaskan Way Viaduct, an elevated highway constructed above the railway serving the docks.

▲ Today Seattle's downtown waterfront is a popular tourist destination, with hotels, shops, restaurants, bars, an aquarium, and a Ferris wheel. The viaduct was replaced with a tunnel in 2019, creating a generous boulevard connecting the city to the waterfront.

# VANCOUVER

Surrounded by British Columbia's snowcapped North Shore Mountains, the city of Vancouver ranks highly as one of the world's most livable cities. This can perhaps be attributed to "Vancouverism," the city's urban planning and architectural design philosophy, which is characterized by medium-height, mixed-use developments with an emphasis on good public transport, open green space, and "view corridors" to protect the city's scenic backdrop. The area was home to the Squamish, Musqueam, and Tsleil-Waututh people for thousands of years until Europeans arrived in the 1800s and turned it into a sawmilling settlement. Today, the city is fast emerging as a global tech hub, as well as a popular location for film and television productions.

◄ Vancouver City, as seen from Fairview, British Columbia, in 1904. The city's sawmills dominated the downtown waterfront area, while the North Shore Mountains loomed high over the city.

▼ Today Vancouver is a thriving coastal city, a popular place both to live in and to visit. The downtown area, now a vibrant foodie and shopping scene, is also home to art galleries and public libraries.

**PACIFIC CENTRAL STATION** Vancouver's impressive Beaux Arts–style Pacific Central Station was designed and built in 1919 by Pratt and Ross Architects for the Canadian Northern Railway. Featuring Doric columns on the exterior and ornate ceiling moldings on the interior, the building has since remained largely unchanged and was declared a designated heritage railway station in 1991.

▲ Top: The station, as seen in 1925, soon after its completion. It was built using granite, brick, and andesite, a volcanic rock sourced from a quarry on nearby Haddington Island. Bottom: The large neon "Pacific Central" sign was added to the station in the 1950s, at the time making it one of Vancouver's most prominent landmarks.

**CHINATOWN** Chinese immigrants began settling what is now Vancouver's Chinatown in the late nineteenth century. They were attracted to British Columbia, initially by the 1858 gold rush and then, in the 1880s, to work on the construction of the Canadian Pacific Railway. This area, which sits between Gastown and Downtown Eastside, has since become Canada's largest Chinatown and has many notable buildings.

▲ Top left: The temporary Welcome Arch, created in 1901 to celebrate the visit of the then Duke and Duchess of Cornwall and York. Bottom left: The towering Millennium Gate that sits at the entrance to Vancouver's Chinatown and was built in 2002 to honor the people of China.

▲ Top right: Pender Street, Chinatown, as seen ca. 1935. The area became known for its distinctive "recessed balcony" that blended Chinese and American architecture styles. Bottom right: Many of Pender Street's colorful buildings remain the same today.

**GASTOWN** Named for its founder, John Deighton, who was better known as "Gassy Jack," Gastown was Vancouver's first settlement. As the city's oldest area, it is classed as a national historic site and retains many of its cobbled streets and an abundance of architecturally distinctive elements, not least its famous steam-powered clock.

▶ Top: "Maple Tree" corner at Water Street, as seen in 1886, where, historically, town meetings and performances were held. Today the area is known as Maple Tree Square. Bottom: Just a few blocks from Maple Tree Square sits Gastown's famous steam-powered clock. Built in 1877, it is one of only a handful of working steam-powered clocks in existence.

**GRANVILLE STREET BRIDGE** First built in 1889, Vancouver's Granville Street Bridge has seen several incarnations. Originally a long, low, timber trestle bridge, in 1909 it was rebuilt using steel, creating a longer, higher structure. The current bridge was constructed in 1954.

▼ Top left: The original timber structure featured a drawbridge to allow ships to pass through. Top right: The second steel incarnation was short-lived, as the city soon outgrew it and a third, bigger bridge was required. Bottom: Today, the Granville Street Bridge, built in 1954, features eight lanes and has since undergone significant retrofitting to help it withstand earthquakes.

**FALSE CREEK** Up until the 1960s, False Creek was the thriving industrial heartland of Vancouver. However, a shift in location of industry within the city led to the eventual decline of the area until the 1980s, when it was revamped and transformed into what it is today, a clean and vibrant neighborhood with very few remnants of its industrial past.

▼  False Creek, as seen here in the 1940s, was the center of industry in the city and home to its many sawmills as well as rail depots and shipyards.

▼ The transformation of False Creek has proved to be a hugely successful urban regeneration project. Today, the area is almost unrecognizable with its abundance of residential housing, restaurants, bars, and shopping areas.

# LAS VEGAS

Billed as the Entertainment Capital of the World, Las Vegas, or simply Vegas, as it is commonly known, is home to some of the largest, most luxurious casinos and hotels ever built. Set deep in Nevada's Mojave Desert, the city is visited by millions of people each year, who go there to enjoy its almost unrivaled nightlife. The area has a long and rich history that dates back thousands of years, having originally been inhabited by the

Southern Paiute people. It was in the 1930s, and then during the subsequent booms of the 1960s and 1990s, that the city really began to grow into what it is today: the gambling capital of the world. Hot, dry, and surrounded by impressive mountains, canyons, and state parks, this twenty-four-hour city is said to have an estimated 15,000 miles of neon lights, making it one of the brightest cities on earth.

◄ **Dunes Hotel, 1967.** Opening in 1955, the Dunes was the tenth resort built on the Las Vegas Strip. The complex was hugely popular and expanded extensively over the years until it closed in the early 1990s.

▼ **Today, Las Vegas** is home to some of the biggest, glitziest hotels and casinos in the world, including the Bellagio, famed for its huge water fountains, which span more than 1,000 feet and shoot water as high as 460 feet into the air.

CITIES PAST AND PRESENT

**FREMONT STREET** Marking the birthplace of Las Vegas, Fremont Street sits north of the Strip, in the downtown area of the city. It was the main street through the area before the city was even founded. Once Vegas took off, it quickly became home to the many famous neon signs that adorned the first casinos.

▼ Fremont Street, 1956. Some of the earliest casinos in Vegas opened on Fremont Street, including the Lucky Strike Club, Bird Cage, and the Golden Nugget, the last of which is still standing today.

▼ Fremont Street, 2019. Suffering from a downturn
due to the popularity of the Las Vegas Strip,
Fremont Street was modernized in 1994, with
a five-block stretch of the street pedestrianized.

## LAS VEGAS STRIP

The Las Vegas Strip, or simply the Strip, runs for just over four miles and is home to some of the biggest casinos and hotels in the world. The architectural theme here is "go big or go home," with many of the area's resorts boasting extravagant designs and a multitude of bright lights.

▲◀ Flamingo hotel, ca. 1950. When the Flamingo hotel complex opened in 1946, it was billed as the first luxury hotel on the Strip, boasting multiple facilities that included a golf course, nightclub, casino, and restaurant.

▶ The hotel was rebuilt over the course of many years beginning in the 1970s, and in 2018 underwent a complete makeover. Today it remains the oldest resort on the Strip that is still in operation.

# CHICAGO

Renowned for its modern architecture, many museums, public art, and vibrant food scene, Chicago is the United States' third-largest city. Sitting on the shores of Lake Michigan, much of the city was destroyed by the Great Chicago Fire of 1871. However, this disaster subsequently led to one of the biggest building booms the country has ever seen and also set a precedent for construction worldwide with the creation, in 1885, of the world's first skyscraper using a steel skeleton frame. To this day, the city of Chicago is still home to

some of the world's tallest buildings and skyscrapers, including the Willis Tower (formerly the Sears Tower), the Trump International Hotel and Tower, St. Regis Chicago, and the Aon Center. The city was also home to the first Ferris wheel, which opened in 1893. Today, a 200-foot-tall Ferris wheel stands on the city's Navy Pier in honor of the original.

◄ **Lake Shore Drive on Chicago's waterfront, as it was in the 1940s. The Drake Hotel can be seen in the foreground, with the Palmolive Building to its rear.**

▼ **Today, Lake Shore Drive's original buildings are overshadowed by the influx of skyscrapers in the city, among them the John Hancock Center, which can be seen here looming behind the Palmolive Building.**

**CHICAGO RIVER** The city of Chicago is situated on the Chicago River, a system of rivers and canals that runs throughout the city for a combined length of 156 miles, and which is crossed by thirty-eight movable bridges. Some of the city's most iconic buildings and skyscrapers line the banks of the waterways, among the first of which was the famous Wrigley Building, completed in 1924. It has since been joined by many others, including the Tribune Tower and 35 East Wacker, also known as the Jewelers Building.

▲ When 35 East Wacker was built in the 1920s, it was the tallest building in the world.

◄ Today, the 35 East Wacker building is somewhat dwarfed by the modern skyscrapers that now surround it in the Loop area of Chicago.

**FEDERAL BUILDING** Chicago's Federal Building was built in the early 1900s, as a place to house the federal courts, post office, and custom house. It was designed in the Beaux Arts style by architect Henry Ives Cobb and was topped with a gilt dome. The building was demolished in 1965 and the area turned into a plaza that housed the much larger Kluczynski Federal Building as part of the then-new Federal Center.

▲ Federal Building, 1905. Cobb based his design on a six-story Greek cross shape with an additional two lower floors in the basement and eight upper floors in an octagonal dome structure. It featured Corinthian columns and eagles perched atop the corbels.

▲ Federal Plaza, 2019. The new Federal Center was created from the late 1950s to the early 1970s and includes the Everett McKinley Dirksen Building, the Kluczynski Federal Building, and the U.S. Post Office–Loop Station. Alexander Calder's *Flamingo* sculpture stands in the plaza.

◄ When the original Federal Building was demolished in the 1960s, two of its Corinthian columns were salvaged and later incorporated into the design of the Cancer Survivors' Garden in nearby Grant Park.

**MILLENNIUM PARK** Having opened in 2004, Millennium Park is in the Loop area of Chicago and sits on the banks of Lake Michigan. The wide-open green space is home to gardens, public art exhibitions, and event venues and is a popular tourist destination. Prior to this, the land was owned by the Illinois Chicago Railroad and was laid with tracks before becoming a baseball ground for the Chicago White Stockings.

▲ The area now known as Millemium Park has been officially designated parkland since 1844. However, the Illinois Central Railroad Company gained the land in 1852 and it became an industrial area, home to railroad tracks and parking lots.

▶ *Cloud Gate*, also known as "The Bean," is the work of British artist Anish Kapoor and sits in the shadow of Chicago's Legacy skyscrapers at Millennium Park.

# NEW ORLEANS

Affectionately known as the Big Easy, New Orleans is home to a melting pot of cultures and is famed for its buzzing twenty-four-hour nightlife, thriving music scene, countless festivals and celebrations, and world-famous Creole cuisine. Sitting on the Mississippi River, the city has a long and rich history, having originally been founded by the French in 1718, before coming under American rule in the early 1800s.

Today, the historic French Quarter remains at the heart of the city with its French Creole architecture and vibrant nightlife enjoyed by millions of residents and visitors each year. More broadly, the city serves as a major port and economic hub for the southern United States. New Orleans is known as the birthplace of jazz and held its first Mardi Gras celebration in the 1800s.

◀ Aerial view of New Orleans, September 2005. Seen here is the New Orleans Superdome in the aftermath of the category 4 Hurricane Katrina, which devastated large parts of the city and left thousands of people displaced.

▼ Aerial view of New Orleans, September 2018. Now known as the Caesars Superdome, the stadium has undergone significant renovations since the hurricane and continues to play host to some of the biggest sporting events in the United States, including the Super Bowl.

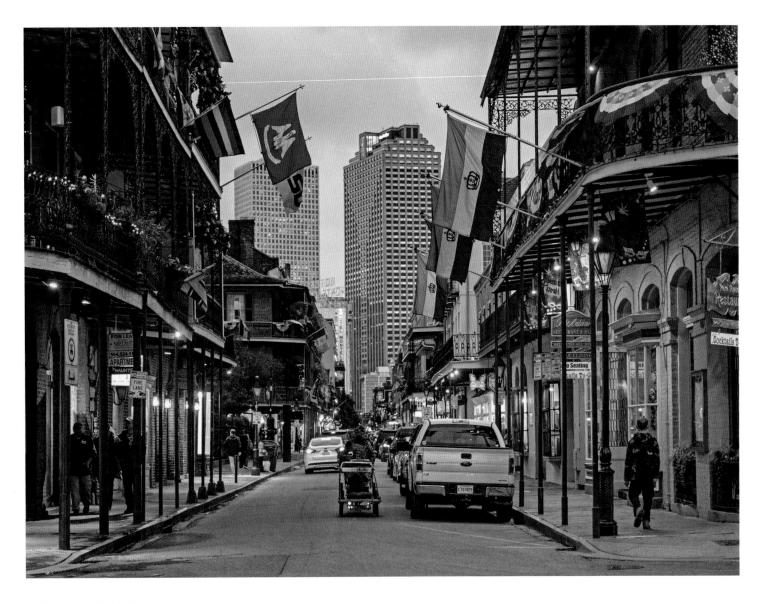

**THE FRENCH QUARTER** New Orleans's oldest neighborhood remains the historic heart of the city, and is home to jazz clubs, bars, Cajun eateries, food markets, and street performers. The distinctive French Creole architecture of the area is also a popular draw for visitors, with its single-story cottages and rows of streets lined with townhouses with pretty cast-iron balconies.

◀ Royal Street, 1960s. Dating back to the early eighteenth century, Royal Street was built on high ground alongside a bend in the Mississippi River. The ornate wrought-iron balcony railings are typical of French Creole architectural style.

▲ Today, Royal Street is home to antiques shops, art galleries, and opulent hotels, as well as being a popular location for musical and street performances. Many of the original balconies remain.

**CANAL STREET** The city's first main thoroughfare, Canal Street is famed for the festivals and parades it has hosted since the mid-1800s, among them the city's world-famous Mardi Gras. Some of New Orleans's oldest and best-known theaters line the street—the Joy, the Orpheum, and the Saenger—as well as upmarket hotels, the Ritz Carlton and the Sheraton.

◀ Canal Street, ca. 1907. This broad (171-foot-wide) and bustling street dates back to 1807. Historically, it was a place for people to gather and celebrate.

◀ The shopping and entertainment district of Canal Street borders the historic French Quarter and the New Orleans modern business district. The city's distinctive red streetcars run the length of the street.

**LOWER NINTH WARD** Originally developed as sugarcane plantations, the Lower Ninth Ward area of New Orleans came to international attention when it was devastated in the wake of Hurricane Katrina in 2005. It took several years for the area to recover, with many homes and businesses rebuilt and renovated. The Lower Ninth Ward was hit again by Hurricane Ida in 2021, although the damage was not on the scale of that caused by Hurricane Katrina.

▲ Work begins on rebuilding a levee that breached during Hurricane Katrina on the Industrial Canal in the Lower Ninth Ward. Most of the area was destroyed by the 2005 hurricane.

▶ Due to significant improvements made to the city's levees, new homes built along the Industrial Canal in the Lower Ninth Ward were able to survive the force of Hurricane Ida in 2021.

**JACKSON SQUARE** This historic park in the heart of the French Quarter is named for Andrew Jackson, a general in the Battle of New Orleans (1815) and later U.S. president. It is home to St. Louis Cathedral to the north, with the Jackson equestrian statue sitting at its center. The square's design is inspired by that of the seventeenth-century Place des Vosges in Paris.

▼ Jackson Square in the late 1800s, with St. Louis Cathedral at the center. The buildings on either side, the Cabildo (right) and the Presbytère (left), once served as a city hall and a courthouse, respectively. Both are now part of the Louisiana State Museum.

▶ The square has long been a popular gathering place for painters and other artists, and in recent years for musicians, street performers, and fortune tellers.

# PHILADELPHIA

The city of Philadelphia, often simply referred to as Philly, played a central role in modern American history as the meeting place of the country's Founding Fathers. Prior to that, it had a long and rich history as the home of the Lenape people, who lived on the land for thousands of years until they were forced out when America was colonized. One of the oldest American cities, Philadelphia was founded in 1682 by an English Quaker named William Penn. The city developed

a thriving textile manufacturing industry in the late 1600s and later, in the 1800s, became one of the earliest major railroad hubs in the United States. Today the city is known for its place at the center of higher education, as well as for its famous architecture and historic landmarks, among them the Liberty Bell, Independence Hall, the Benjamin Franklin Bridge, and Philadelphia City Hall.

◄  **Aerial view of Philadelphia, ca. 1930. The city was built on a grid system, with the mile-long Benjamin Franklin Parkway running diagonally through its cultural heart.**

▼  **Today, Philadelphia's skyline is defined by a number of landmark skyscrapers that include the Comcast Technology Center, the Comcast Center, and Three Logan Square.**

**BENJAMIN FRANKLIN PARKWAY** Known locally
as the Parkway, Benjamin Franklin Parkway was named
for one of America's Founding Fathers. The tree-lined
boulevard runs from Philadelphia City Hall to the
Philadelphia Museum of Art, curving around historic
Logan Circle en route. It is one of the earliest examples
of successful urban renewal, having been created to ease
congestion in the city center.

▼ Benjamin Franklin Parkway, 1950s. The boulevard was built
as part of the City Beautiful movement, an architectural and
urban-planning scheme popular in the late nineteenth and
early twentieth centuries, which aimed to make American
cities grander and more beautiful.

▶ The Washington Monument Fountain sits to the north of the
boulevard. Today, views down to Philadelphia City Hall are
somewhat dwarfed by the city's modern skyscrapers.

# WASHINGTON, D.C.

As the capital of the United States, Washington, D.C., is known for such famous buildings and monuments as the White House, the Capitol Building, the Lincoln Memorial, and the Supreme Court Building. Situated on the east bank of the Potomac River, the city as it is known today was established in 1790 and named for one of America's Founding Fathers, and its first president, George Washington. A "planned city," Washington was created using a grid system

based on the plans of cities such as Milan, Paris, and Amsterdam. It is famed for its unique architecture, with many of the city's significant buildings inspired by Neoclassical, Georgian, and Gothic architectural styles. Among the most notable are Washington National Cathedral and the Thomas Jefferson Memorial.

◄ **Aerial view of Washington, 1930s.** Washington's grid system is divided into four quadrants—Northwest, Northeast, Southwest, and Southeast—with Capitol Hill at the center.

▼ **Aerial view of Washington, 2007.** Washington's Capitol Hill, site of the Senate and House office buildings, the Supreme Court Building, the Library of Congress, the Washington Navy Yard, and the Marine Barracks.

## WASHINGTON MONUMENT

The obelisk that sits within the National Mall took a staggering forty years to complete. It was the world's tallest building when it was finally finished in 1884, but was surpassed by the building of the Eiffel Tower in Paris in 1889. Built from granite, the obelisk stands 555 feet tall and is faced with two kinds of Maryland marble. For those wishing to take in the view from the top, there is an observation deck, reached by stairs (897 steps) or elevator.

◄◄ In the summer of 1963, more than 200,000 demonstrators took part in the March on Washington for Jobs and Freedom, to protest against racial discrimination and show support for civil rights legislation.

◄ "I Have a Dream" are the words inscribed on the steps of the Lincoln Memorial. They mark the spot where, in 1963, Dr. Martin Luther King Jr. stood while making one of his most famous speeches.

**CAPITOL BUILDING** An impressive example of nineteenth-century Neoclassical-style architecture, the Capitol Building consists of 540 rooms and miles of corridors. Construction began in the late 1700s, but progress was slow. The building was partly damaged by the fires of the 1814 burning of Washington, and then subsequently restored and expanded with further wings and chambers added. The building that stands today was finally completed in the late 1860s.

▶ Top: In 1856, the original dome was removed and work began on a new cast-iron dome in a "wedding cake style." Center: The new dome was not completed until 1866, work having been interrupted by the Civil War. Bottom: On top of the dome stands the bronze *Statue of Freedom*.

**LINCOLN MEMORIAL** Built to honor the sixteenth president of the United States, Abraham Lincoln, the Lincoln Memorial sits on Washington's National Mall between the Capitol Building and the Washington Monument. Built in marble, in the style of a classic Greek temple, the memorial is surrounded by thirty-six fluted Doric columns above which each of the names of the thirty-six states of America (at the time of Lincoln's death) are inscribed.

◀ The Lincoln Memorial with its Reflecting Pool as seen during the March on Washington for Jobs and Freedom in 1963, and then in the present day.

▲ On the inside of the memorial sits a large seated statue of Lincoln and inscriptions of two of his best-known speeches, the Gettysburg Address and his second inaugural address.

# NEW YORK

Hailed as the city that never sleeps, New York, or the Big Apple as it is affectionately known, is renowned for its nonstop, twenty-four-hour nightlife, iconic skyscrapers, high-profile galleries and museums, and many public parks and green spaces. It has landmarks and monuments that are among the most recognized sights in the world, including the Statue of Liberty, the Empire State Building, Times Square, and the Brooklyn Bridge. Sitting on a large natural harbor, the

modern-day city was founded as a trading post by the Dutch in the late 1600s and quickly grew into a major economic center. Before that, the land on which it sits was occupied for thousands of years by the Lenape people, who knew their territory as Lenapehoking. Today, the city that we now know as New York remains an economic and cultural hub and is one of the most visited cities in the world, as well as one of the most photographed.

◄ **The USS *Akron*, the U.S. Navy's helium-filled aircraft carrier, flies over Lower Manhattan in the 1930s, with the city's many ports visible on the banks of the East and Hudson Rivers.**

▼ **Today, Lower Manhattan is populated with some of the world's tallest skyscrapers, including One World Trade Center, which stands at an impressive 1,776 feet tall.**

**GRAND CENTRAL TERMINAL** Manhattan's Grand Central Terminal is the largest train station in the world. Rebuilt three times, the iteration we see today opened to the public in 1913 and is both an architectural and an engineering masterpiece. Designed in the Beaux Arts style by architects Reed and Stem and Warren and Wetmore, one of its more unusual features is a whispering gallery on the lower floor.

▲ The first iteration of the station opened in 1871 as the Grand Central Depot. It was then reconstructed, expanded, and renamed Grand Central Station in 1900, before being entirely replaced by the current building.

▶ The construction of the new Grand Central Terminal was huge in scale and resulted in the creation of the largest terminus in the world, both in terms of size of building and number of platforms.

**TIMES SQUARE** Originally known as Longacre Square, Times Square was renamed as such when the *New York Times* moved its offices to the newly built Times Building (now One Times Square) in 1904. Famed for its illuminated billboards, hugely popular New Year's Eve ball drop, and close proximity to the theaters of Broadway, Times Square is one of the busiest, and most visited, pedestrian areas on earth, often referred to as the Crossroads of the World.

◀ Times Square, 1919. Once the center for the horse-and-carriage industry, by the late nineteenth century Times Square began its transition to becoming the heart of the city's busy theater and entertainment industry.

◀ Times Square, 2018. Built in a neo-Gothic style in 1904, One Times Square has been heavily modified over the years. Today it is almost entirely covered in illuminated advertising screens.

**FLATIRON BUILDING** New York's much-loved Flatiron Building is said to be one of the first buildings to have been constructed using a steel skeleton. Built in three horizontal sections, creating a distinctive triangular shape, at its narrowest point the building is just six and a half feet wide. It was built in this way to fit the wedge-shaped piece of land on which it sits at the intersection of Broadway and Fifth Avenue.

◄ Designed in the Beaux Arts style by architects Daniel Burnham and Frederick P. Dinkelberg, the Flatiron Building was constructed in 1902. Its base is clad with limestone, with the upper floors in glazed terra cotta.

► One of New York's oldest surviving skyscrapers today, the Flatiron Building takes its name from its resemblance to the clothing irons in use at the time of its construction.

**BROOKLYN BRIDGE** Spanning the East River from Brooklyn to Manhattan, the Brooklyn Bridge is an impressive example of engineering and the first bridge to be built using steel for cable wire. Designed by civil engineer John Augustus Roebling, the bridge took fourteen years to build, opening to the public in 1883.

▲ A hybrid cable-stayed suspension structure, the Brooklyn Bridge's most distinctive features are its two huge neo-Gothic stone arch towers built from limestone and granite.

◀ To separate cars from pedestrians, the bridge was designed to include a large raised walkway above its roadway. A dedicated bikeway was added to the bridge in 2021.

# MIAMI

Lined with white sandy beaches and crystal-clear blue waters, Miami is possibly best known for its nonstop party lifestyle, but it also has a thriving finance industry and is one of the United States' biggest ports. Situated on a peninsula with the Biscayne Bay to the east and the Everglades to the west, Miami was originally the home of the Tequesta people, who are said to have lived in a village at the mouth of what is now known as

the Miami River, before the area was colonized by the Spanish in the 1560s. It became part of the United States in the early 1800s. Architecturally, Miami is famed for having the world's highest concentration of Art Deco buildings, and it is these that give the South Beach skyline its distinct colorful look. In all, there are more than 800 Art Deco structures within the city's one-square-mile Art Deco Historic District.

◀ South Beach, Miami, early 1900s. Prior to development, the area on which South Beach now sits was desolate farmland. By the 1920s, however, it was established as a resort community.

▼ Miami is known as the Magic City due to its speed of growth. With more than 300 high-rise buildings, it ranks third after New York and Chicago as the United States' tallest city.

**COLLINS AVENUE** A prime shopping district, Collins Avenue is also known for some of the city's most luxurious hotels. Many of the landmark buildings here were constructed between 1920 and 1965 and form the heart of the city's Art Deco Historic District.

▲ The Delano Hotel is one of South Beach's most exclusive hotels. Built in 1947, it was originally designed by architect Robert Swartburg. In 1994 it underwent extensive renovations led by French designer Philippe Starck.

▶ The Di Lido was another much-loved Art Deco–style hotel, designed by architect Morris Lapidus in 1953. Today it is part of the Ritz-Carlton group of hotels.

**FREEDOM TOWER** Designed by Schultze and Weaver, Miami's Freedom Tower opened in 1925, and for many years the *Miami News* was printed here. Architecturally, the design is of Mediterranean Revival style with a distinctly decorated cupola. Today, the Museum of Art and Design and a gallery that hosts exhibitions celebrating Cuban culture occupy space in the tower, which also functions as a cultural and education center as part of Miami Dade College.

▲◀ Cuban American businessman Jorge Mas Conosa bought the Freedom Tower in 1997. He restored it and converted it into a memorial to those who fled to the United States from Cuba, as well as making it home to the offices of the Cuban American National Foundation.

▲ During the 1960s, the Freedom Tower was used by the U.S. government to process Cuban refugees. In 2008, the tower was designated a U.S. National Historic Landmark.

# BUENOS AIRES

The capital city of Argentina, Buenos Aires has a rich and vibrant history and culture. Famed for its ornate, European-style architecture, wide, tree-lined avenues—among them the world's widest, Avenida 9 de Julio, at 459 feet—and old cobbled streets, Buenos Aires is also known as the Paris of South America. Situated on the shores of the Río de la Plata, the city as we know it today was first settled by the Spanish in the 1500s and quickly became a center for trade. It remains the financial and commercial hub of Argentina and its port is one of South America's busiest. Buenos Aires also lays claim to the most bookshops per capita in the world. Among them, El Ateneo Grand Splendid is considered the most beautiful.

◄ Plaza del Congreso, 1900. Designed by architect Victor Meano, Buenos Aires's monumental parliament building, the Palacio del Congreso, took nearly fifty years to complete. It was inaugurated in 1906, but work then continued for another forty years.

▼ Plaza del Congreso, present day. Largely constructed using limestone and topped with a 260-foot-high bronze-plated dome, the design of the Palacio del Congreso was modeled on the United States Capitol Building in Washington, D.C.

## PLAZA DE MAYO
Buenos Aires's Plaza de Mayo has long been associated with political life in Argentina. Its name commemorates the May 1810 revolution, which eventually led to the country's independence from Spain. While its origins can be traced back to 1580, the modern-day plaza began life in 1884. Located in the financial district of the city, the plaza has played host to some of the largest demonstrations in the country.

▲ Pictured here in 1900, the Plaza de Mayo is the oldest public square in Buenos Aires. The obelisk was built in 1811 and marks the spot where the rebellion that triggered Argentina's march to independence began.

◄ Today, the plaza is a major tourist attraction containing several of the city's major landmarks, including the presidential office of the Casa Rosada (aka the Pink House), the Metropolitan Cathedral, and the Cabildo—a former town hall that is now a museum.

**PUERTO MADERO** This waterfront area of Buenos Aires sits on the Río de la Plata riverbank. As the city's first port, it dates back to the late 1800s when local businessman Eduardo Madero oversaw its construction. However, with the arrival of larger ships the port soon became unusable and, in 1926, the more accommodating Puerto Nuevo was built nearby. That port is still in operation today.

▲ It took ten years to build the Puerto Madero; at the time it was considered an engineering masterpiece. It operated as the principal port in Argentina for around thirty years before the advent of larger ships made it obsolete.

▶ After being neglected for some years, the old redbrick warehouse buildings of Puerto Madero were revitalized and now house popular upscale restaurants, shops, and offices in this once-again thriving area.

# RIO DE JANEIRO

Sitting on Guanabara Bay, surrounded by steep, forest-covered mountains, the city of Rio de Janeiro is the jewel in Brazil's crown. Fondly known as the Marvelous City, it is famed for its natural beauty, glittering Carnival, the gigantic *Christ the Redeemer* statue that sits atop Mount Corcovado in the Tijuca National Park, and for being the birthplace of samba. It is also home to the biggest urban rain forest in the world (Floresta da Tijuca) as well as the famous Sugarloaf Mountain and around fifty miles of pristine white sandy beaches including Copacabana and Ipanema.

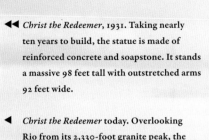

◀◀ *Christ the Redeemer*, 1931. Taking nearly
ten years to build, the statue is made of
reinforced concrete and soapstone. It stands
a massive 98 feet tall with outstretched arms
92 feet wide.

◀ *Christ the Redeemer* today. Overlooking
Rio from its 2,330-foot granite peak, the
majestic statue attracts nearly 2 million
visitors a year.

◀▼ Opposite bottom: Botafogo Cove,
Guanabara Bay, ca. 1880, with
Corcovado Mountain in the background.

▼ Aerial view of Rio de Janeiro today, with
Corcovado Mountain rising high above
Flamengo and Botafogo beaches.

# LONDON

London is one of the world's oldest cities, with a rich history that can be traced back almost 2,000 years. Founded by the Romans, occupied by the Saxons, invaded by the Vikings, destroyed by a devastating fire, and heavily bombed during both world wars, today London is a sprawling modern metropolis. The city stands on the banks of the river Thames and is renowned for its thriving arts, entertainment, and fashion

industries, as well as acting as a global financial hub. Known for its mix of ancient and modern architecture, the city is home to four UNESCO World Heritage Sites and many world-famous landmarks, including the Tower of London, the Palace of Westminster with its Big Ben clock tower, St. Paul's Cathedral, and the London residence of the reigning monarch, Buckingham Palace.

◄ Officially called the Palace of Westminster but more commonly known as the Houses of Parliament, this is the meeting place for members of the House of Commons and House of Lords. It sits on the banks of the Thames.

▼ Built in the mid-1800s in the Gothic Revival style, today the building remains largely unchanged. Regular upkeep means that the adjoining 180-year-old clock, known as Big Ben, still chimes every fifteen minutes.

▲  Top left: London in the first days of the
Blitz, September 9, 1940. The German
bombing raids damaged or destroyed
1.1 million houses and apartments across
the city, and killed 43,000 civilians.
Top right: Harrington Square, North
London. It took many years to rebuild
some areas of the city.

**LONDON BLITZ** Beginning on September 7, 1940, during World War II, the Blitz was a sustained aerial bombing campaign by the German Luftwaffe across British towns and cities. London was bombed the most heavily, starting with fifty-seven consecutive nights. The raids lasted until May 11, 1941, leaving thousands dead and injured and destroying numerous buildings and landmarks throughout the city.

▲ Top: The view along Watling Street in London after an overnight air raid in May 1941. The dome of St. Paul's Cathedral can be seen in the distance. Bottom: Although its dome was pierced by a bomb on one occasion, the centuries-old cathedral escaped major damage during the Blitz.

**TOWER BRIDGE** Opening in 1894, London's Tower Bridge is known for its striking neo-Gothic design and central "drawbridge" sections. Its combined bascule and suspension bridge design, complete with two ornate towers and upper walkways, was the brainchild of architect Horace Jones, who worked alongside engineer John Wolfe Barry. It took eight years to construct, and crosses the river Thames a short distance from London Bridge.

◀ Construction of the Tower Bridge in stages, 1894. Built to meet the demand of increasing commercial development in East London, when it opened, the Tower Bridge was the most sophisticated bridge in the world. The pair of central bascules lift up to allow tall ships to pass through.

▼ Originally powered by hydraulics, the bridge's operating mechanisms were switched to an electro-hydraulic system in 1972. The towers, upper walkways, and engine rooms are now open to the public as part of a permanent exhibition.

**GREENWICH PARK** Originally heathland, today Greenwich Park is one of London's largest and oldest enclosed parks. Set on a hilltop just south of the river Thames, it is part of the Greenwich World Heritage Site. Its historic buildings include the Royal Observatory, the Old Royal Naval College, the National Maritime Museum, and Queen's House. The prime meridian passes through the Royal Observatory and is the north–south line representing longitude zero. Greenwich

▲ Queen's House, ca. 1950. Commissioned by Queen Anne and designed by architect Inigo Jones, the Palladian-style house was a design masterpiece. The original building was constructed in 1635 with additional wings, linked by colonnades, added in 1807.

has always had strong connections to the monarchy, having been the birthplace of Henry VIII in 1491. King Henry introduced deer to the park, which he and Queen Elizabeth I used as a hunting ground. Landscaped in the seventeenth century and opened to the public in the eighteenth century, today the park is a popular destination for Londoners and tourists alike.

▲ Queen's House, 2019. Today, it is one of the Royal Museums Greenwich and is somewhat overshadowed by the skyscrapers of London's second-largest financial district, Canary Wharf, which loom large behind it.

# PARIS

Paris has several names, among the most popular being the City of Love, the City of Light, and the Fashion Capital of the World. Set on a bend in the river Seine that flows through the heart of the city, Paris has it all—art, fashion, music, architecture, and history. It is also world-famous for its outstanding cuisine. Dating as far back as the third century BC, this popular commercial trading center was conquered by the Romans in 52 BC, but came under the rule of the first king of

the Franks, Clovis I, in AD 508, when he made the city his capital. Among the city's many famous landmarks are the Louvre—the world's largest art gallery—Notre-Dame cathedral, the Sacré-Coeur Basilica, the Arc de Triomphe, the Eiffel Tower, and the more modern Centre Pompidou. The city is also famed for its many pretty tree-lined boulevards and its popular public parks, gardens, and squares.

◄ Aerial view of Paris, 1930s. At the western end of the Champs-Élysées stands the Arc de Triomphe, a formidable structure built in 1836 to honor those who fought and died for France in the French Revolutionary and Napoleonic Wars.

▼ Aerial view of Paris, 2018. Positioned at the center of the starlike Place Charles de Gaulle, the Neoclassical Arc de Triomphe was designed by Jean Chalgrin. Beneath the arch is the tomb of an unknown soldier from World War I.

**NOTRE-DAME** Notre-Dame de Paris, which translates as Our Lady of Paris, is one of the most famous French Gothic cathedrals in the world. Built between 1163 and 1345, initially under the reign of King Louis VII, this architectural marvel sits on the Île de la Cité, a small island in the middle of the Seine. The cathedral is home to many Gothic and Baroque sculptures, as well as a number of seventeenth- and eighteenth-century altarpieces.

◀▲ Notre-Dame, ca. 1860. Construction of the cathedral began in 1163 and was completed over 200 years. Many additions and modifications have been made since.

◀ Not just for decoration, the thirty-nine gargoyles atop the cathedral serve as part of a water drainage system helping to direct rainwater away from the cathedral walls.

▲ Famed for its breathtaking stained-glass windows, towering spires, and intricate stone carvings, Notre-Dame cathedral has survived numerous wars and revolutions and today is a designated UNESCO World Heritage Site.

▶ In April 2019, the cathedral was hit by a fire that destroyed much of the building, including its roof and spire. It has since been closed for restoration work.

**EIFFEL TOWER** Built as the centerpiece for the 1889 Exposition Universelle, the Eiffel Tower, often referred to as *la dame de fer* (iron lady), is one of the most recognizable buildings in the world. When the 1,083-foot-tall tower was built, it surpassed the Washington Monument to become the tallest structure in the world—a title it held for just over forty years, until the Chrysler Building in New York took its place in 1930.

▲ Construction of the tower began in early 1887. Concrete foundations were laid on which the intricate wrought-iron structure was built. Sections of the tower were built in a nearby factory and brought on site for assembly.

▶ Over the course of the build, nearly 20,000 drawings were produced, mapping out how the lattice structure was to be constructed. The finished tower consisted of 18,038 parts joined together using 2.5 million rivets.

▶▶ Today, the Eiffel Tower is the most visited paid monument in the world with around 25,000 visitors passing through each day. As well as a viewing platform, the tower is also home to two restaurants and a single apartment.

# ROME

Dating back nearly 3,000 years, Rome is one of Europe's oldest continuously inhabited cities. It gets its name, City of Seven Hills, from the group of hills on which the ancient city was built. Today, these hills mark the boundaries of that ancient city. Sitting on the Tiber River, Rome was one of the first major centers of the Renaissance, and thanks to a succession of popes who wanted to make the city the artistic and cultural

center of the world, architectural wonders abound. Among the most impressive are St. Peter's Basilica, the Tempietto, the Sistine Chapel, and Piazza del Campidoglio. Rome was the birthplace of the Baroque and Neoclassical styles of art and architecture, and many renowned painters, sculptors, musicians, and architects are associated with the city, including Michelangelo and Caravaggio.

◀ **St. Peter's Basilica, 1916. Located in the Vatican City, this is one of the best-known works of Renaissance architecture in the world. Construction on the building started in 1506 and was completed in 1626.**

▼ **St. Peter's Basilica, present day. The largest church in the world, the basilica features many Baroque elements. It sits on Piazza di San Pietro, where its central dome dominates the Rome skyline.**

## COLOSSEUM AND ARCH OF CONSTANTINE

Built in AD 80, and with a capacity of more than 50,000 people, Rome's Colosseum is the largest amphitheater ever built. Sitting close by is the Arch of Constantine, which was built in AD 315 to commemorate Emperor Constantine the Great's victory over the then-reigning Emperor Maxentius.

◀ Built during the reigns of the Flavian emperors, the Colosseum was constructed using limestone, volcanic rock, and concrete. In its heyday, the amphitheater played host to gladiatorial games as well as dramas and wild animal fights.

▶ Located between the Palatine and Caelian Hills in ancient Rome, this triple triumphal arch signified Constantine's victory in the civil war of 312, which cemented his position as ruler of the Roman Empire.

# BERLIN

A city with a turbulent past, Germany's capital, Berlin, sits in the northeast of the country on the banks of the river Spree. The earliest settlement here can be traced back to the 1100s, before it became the capital of Margraviate of Brandenburg under the Holy Roman Empire. It later became Brandenburg-Prussia, as part of the Kingdom of Prussia, before finally becoming part of the German Empire in 1817. For nearly three decades, from the early 1960s to the late 1980s, the city was divided into East and West by the Berlin Wall.

Today, Berlin is a melting pot of history, art, music, and creativity. This now thriving city is known for its countless museums and galleries (including the longest open-air gallery in the world, the East Side Gallery), historic landmarks, and world-famous nightlife, as well as its many vast and open public green spaces and revitalized waterways.

◄ The Reichstag, 1933. Opening in 1894, Berlin's parliamentary building was destroyed by fire in 1933, possibly by the Nazis so that Hitler could seize power. The building was also heavily bombed during World War II.

▼ The Reichstag today. Having fallen into disrepair after World War II, it was only after the reunification of Germany in 1990 that the building was restored and once more became the seat of the German parliament.

▲ Border police in front of the Brandenburg Gate and the Berlin Wall, 1987. For almost three decades in the mid-twentieth century, the gate sat within a restricted area of the divided city, with neither East nor West Germans permitted to visit it.

**BRANDENBURG GATE** Berlin's Brandenburg Gate is one of the city's most historically significant landmarks. Built in the eighteenth century, this imposing Neoclassical sandstone structure sits in the Mitte district of modern-day Berlin. In the postwar years, it became a potent symbol of the Cold War and of the division of Berlin—and Germany as a whole—into East and West with the erection of the Berlin Wall in 1961. Twenty-eight years later, the gate also became a symbol of unification when the wall fell in 1989.

▲ Berliners crowd around the Berlin Wall, November 1989. The fall of the wall symbolized not only the end of the Cold War but a new start for the city of Berlin, its two halves now reunited.

◄ Brandenburg Gate, 1945. The Quadriga sitting atop the gate had been placed there in 1793. Both the sculpture and the gate were severely damaged by bombing during World War II.

◄ Now fully restored, the impressive structure stands 66 feet high and 216 feet wide and is supported by twelve Doric columns, creating five portals. The Quadriga is a replica.

**BERLIN CATHEDRAL** The monumental Renaissance and Baroque Revival Berlin Cathedral dates back to the fifteenth century, when it was a Roman Catholic place of worship. Since then it has seen many incarnations, with the present one having been designed by architect Julius Carl Raschdorff by order of German Emperor Wilhelm II and opening to the public in 1905. The cathedral sits on Museum Island in central Berlin.

▲ Berlin Cathedral, 1945. Built between 1894 and 1905, the cathedral's grandiose structure and lavishly decorated inside was in part created as Berlin's answer to St. Peter's in Rome and St. Paul's in London. Its large central dome was all but destroyed by Allied bombing in World War II.

▶ Despite significant damage during World War II, the cathedral has since been restored following its original design. The large central dome is once more crowned with a lantern and golden cross and surrounded by four towers.

▲ Potsdamer Platz, 1945. The station and surrounding building lie in ruins following the continued air raids toward the end of World War II.

◄ Potsdamer Platz, ca. 1935. Berlin's first railway station, at center, opened in the square in 1838, its arrival heralding the beginning of the square's transformation into a bustling trade hub.

**POTSDAMER PLATZ** Having been almost completely destroyed during World War II and then abandoned during the Cold War, Potsdamer Platz public square has undergone something of a revival since the reunification of Germany. The square dates as far back as 1685, when it was used as the central trading post for the city. From there, it grew to become one of the busiest commercial hubs in Europe, until it was all but decimated by repeated bombing in 1945.

▲ **Today Potsdamer Platz is once again a bustling area of the city. A new train station is now dwarfed by some of Berlin's tallest buildings, including the 338-foot-tall Bahn Tower, designed by Helmut Jahn (right), and Hans Kollhof's Potsdamer Platz 11, with its peat-fired brick facade (left).**

# VIENNA

Known as the City of Music, Vienna is the unofficial classical music capital of the world, with both Beethoven and Mozart having called the city home. It lies in northeastern Austria, on the banks of the Danube River, close to the borders of the Czech Republic, Slovakia, and Hungary. Beyond the city limits lie the Vienna Woods, a UNESCO designated Biosphere Reserve in the foothills of the Alps. The city is bursting with museums, theaters, and Baroque palaces, as

well as three world-famous opera houses. Perhaps the best known, the Vienna State Opera, holds an annual ball season of more than 450 balls, many of which run through the night. Among the city's notable historic landmarks are the Schönbrunn Palace, St. Stephen's Cathedral, and the monumental Austrian parliament building. Last but not least is the giant Ferris wheel, the Wiener Riesenrad, captured beautifully in the 1949 film noir masterpiece *The Third Man*.

◄ Aerial view of the city, 1945. The historical center of Vienna is compact and little changed over the centuries. This view across the city was taken from St. Stephen's Cathedral, following a fire that damaged the building at the end of World War II.

▼ The same view across the city, seen today. Little has changed, and St. Stephen's Cathedral continues to dominate the skyline. The green dome in the distance is that of the early eighteenth-century St. Peter's Church.

**KOHLMARKT** This small street in the heart of Vienna's first district is the most expensive shopping street in the city. Lined with historic buildings and high-end shops, this busy pedestrian area has a long and rich history that can be traced as far back as the early 1300s. The prestigious Dorotheum auction house, established in 1707, can be found here, as can stores for luxury Viennese jewelers Wagner, Bucherer, and Schullin. The composers Joseph Haydn and Frédéric Chopin both lived in houses on this street.

▲◀ Kohlmarkt, 1922. In the distance stands the striking dome of Vienna's Imperial Palace. It was the street's proximity to the palace that led to it being filled with expensive stores.

▲ Today, Kohlmarkt remains popular with locals and visitors alike. In recent years this street, along with neighboring Graben and Kärntner Strasse, have formed a pedestrianized area dubbed the "Golden U."

**VIENNA STATE OPERA** Built in the mid-1800s where Vienna's old city walls used to lie, the Vienna State Opera is an impressive example of Renaissance Revival architecture. However, despite its popularity today, when it first opened it was met with public criticism, described as a "sunken treasure chest." After being significantly damaged during World War II, the building was restored to mirror its original design. Inside, the opulent Schwind Foyer miraculously escaped destruction during the war.

▲▲ The Vienna State Opera, 1945. On March 12, 1945, the building was largely destroyed by a fire that consumed the stage and auditorium, as well as countless props and costumes.

▲ The Vienna State Opera, present day. Restoration of the building was completed in 1955. While large parts of the building were modernized, the original facade, entrance hall, and famous Schwind Foyer had survived destruction.

## ST. STEPHEN'S CATHEDRAL

St. Stephen's Cathedral has a long and rich history that can be traced as far back as 1160. Its structure has been destroyed by fire, rebuilt, bombed, and once again restored to make it what it is today. This masterpiece of ornate Gothic architecture was built using limestone and features many intricate statues. The ornately colored and patterned mosaic roof was created using 230,000 small glazed tiles.

▶ St. Stephen's Cathedral, ca. 1950, with reconstruction work underway. A huge restoration effort following the 1945 fire saw the cathedral reopen to visitors in 1952.

▶▶ Today, the cathedral remains one of old Vienna's tallest buildings, its 450-foot-tall tower offering visitors impressive views across the city.

# CAIRO

Famous for its 4,000-year-old Giza pyramid complex, modern-day Cairo itself dates back around 1,000 years. Sitting on the Nile River, the historic city, known as the City of a Thousand Minarets due to its many mosques, can be dizzying with its narrow streets, bustling markets, and countless museums. Cairo, which in Arabic means "The Victorious One," has long been the region's center of political, financial, and cultural life, as well as being home to one of the world's oldest and biggest statues, the Sphinx. Cairo is also where you will find the Al-Azhar Mosque and University.

▼ The Giza pyramid complex, early 1900s. Built between 2600 and 2500 BC, the three monumental buildings here are the Great Pyramid (Khufu), the Pyramid of Khafre, and the Pyramid of Menkaure.

▶ Today, the city of Cairo has exploded in size and now sprawls close to the famed pyramid complex. For the most part, however, the site remains much as it has for thousands of years.

## MENA HOUSE HOTEL The historic Marriott Mena House Hotel sits in the shadows of the famous great pyramids of Giza, Cairo. Built on the site of an old hunting lodge, the hotel opened in 1887. It is named for King Menes, who was the founding father of the first Egyptian dynasty, ca. 2925 BC.

▲ Mena House Hotel, photographed by Félix Bonfils, ca. 1900. The hotel was designed in the late 1880s by Cairo-based English architect Henri Favarger. He drew inspiration from the architecture of the streets of old Cairo, the hotel featuring multiple recessed sections, terraces, and roof parapets.

▶ Mena House Hotel, today. Four years after it opened, the hotel became the first in Egypt to have a swimming pool—though this has since been upgraded. It also featured a billiards room, artists' studio, library, and photographers' darkroom.

# DUBAI

The city of Dubai began life as a small fishing and pearl-diving village surrounded by desert in the early eighteenth century. Today, it is the eponymous capital of one of the seven emirates that make up the United Arab Emirates on the eastern coast of the Arabian Peninsula. This desert city is home to the tallest building in the world (Burj Khalifa), a shopping mall that claims to have 100 million visitors a year (Dubai Mall), and a manmade island that is visible from space (Palm Jumeirah).

Dubai's incredible transformation over little more than half a century arose from the discovery of oil in the 1960s, which the city used to finance its infrastructure. While the city's newest developments line the Sheikh Zayed Road inland, Dubai's old town, featuring classic Arabic architecture and a traditional souk, sits on the banks of Dubai Creek on the shores of the Persian Gulf.

◀ **Sheikh Zayed Road, 1990. Built between 1971 and 1980, this is the Dubai stretch of the E11 highway that serves as the main artery of the United Arab Emirates. At 347 miles long, it is the region's longest road.**

▼ **Today, following the city's construction boom, Sheikh Zayed Road is lined with some of Dubai's best-known skyscrapers including the Jumeirah Emirates Towers, Park Place Tower, and the Blue Tower.**

**BURJ KHALIFA** Standing an impressive 2,722 feet tall (just over half a mile), Dubai's Burj Khalifa is the tallest building in the world. It was created as the centerpiece of the Downtown Dubai development that also includes shopping malls, entertainment venues, vast public spaces, luxury apartments, and hotels. Designed by Skidmore, Owings & Merrill, the same architects responsible for New York's One World Trade Center and Chicago's Willis Tower, it was created using a bundled tube system.

▲▶ The tower's design takes inspiration from the geometry seen in the *Hymenocallis* spider lily, a regional desert flower, and in patterning systems found in Islamic architecture.

# SINGAPORE

Sitting just off the tip of the Malay Peninsula in Southeast Asia, Singapore, known as the Lion City, is one of only three places in the world that are both a country and a city-state, the other two being Monaco and Vatican City. Consisting of one main island and sixty-three smaller surrounding islands, Singapore is famed for being a modern-day city full of tall skyscrapers. However, it is also one of the greenest cities in the world, thanks to prolific urban planting and many open green spaces. A former colony of the British Empire, Singapore was an important trading post as far back as the fourteenth century. After briefly falling to Japanese and then Malaysian rule, it gained independence in the 1960s and in recent years has emerged as one of the biggest financial hubs in the world.

◀ The mouth of the Singapore River, ca. 1941. To the right stands the prestigious Fullerton Building. Constructed in 1928, it housed Singapore's General Post Office and offices of the governor of Singapore.

▼ That same waterfront area is totally transformed today. In the foreground, the former Fullerton Building, now a hotel, is dwarfed by the skyscrapers of downtown Singapore.

**CHINATOWN** Singapore's Chinatown began as a series of districts in an area west of the Singapore River, established in the early 1800s. Each district was inhabited by people who shared the same dialect—Cantonese or Hokkien, for example. The area grew rapidly from the 1840s and eventually became overcrowded. Many residents were relocated in the 1980s, and the original districts have since been awarded conservation status.

▲◄ Chinatown's Smith Street, 1983, before the forced relocation of the residents of this neighborhood. Smith Street was known locally as "theater street," as the Cantonese opera house was built here in the 1880s.

▲ Smith Street today, having been saved from demolition in the 1980s. The street is better known as "Chinatown Food Street," due to its abundance of restaurants.

## BOAT QUAY SHOPHOUSES

The historic area of Boat Quay was once the city's busiest port and home to its many shophouses. Found in Southeast Asia, a shophouse is a building that has both residential and commercial functions, with a shop opening onto the sidewalk. The majority of the nineteenth-century shophouses at Boat Quay were two-story terraced buildings.

▶ Top: Boat Quay shophouses were two or three stories tall. The ground floor of a shophouse was used for business, while the upper floors were where the shop owners or workers lived. Bottom: With the quay no longer in use as a center for trade, its shophouses have been restored and today are home to a thriving bar and restaurant scene.

# SHANGHAI

Known as the Magic City, Shanghai was once a small agricultural village and market town, but today is the third-largest city in the world and a major financial and cultural center. Translating literally as "City on the Sea," Shanghai is located on the southern estuary of the Yangtze River and is the world's busiest port. With a history spanning thousands of years, Shanghai has a rich cultural heritage as can be seen by its many historic buildings, including the Longhua

Temple and Pagoda and the Jing'an Temple. Numerous Art Deco buildings line the mile-long Bund waterfront, notably the Fairmont Peace Hotel and the Paramount dancehall. The city's ever-changing skyline is known for its skyscrapers, among them the Shanghai Tower, the second-tallest building in the world at just over 2,000 feet tall. They city is also home to many museums and art galleries, as well as the imposing Shanghai Library, one of the largest libraries in the world.

◄ **The Bund area of Shanghai, 1936. Home to numerous international banks and trading houses, this riverside development has operated as a financial center since the early twentieth century.**

▼ **Many of the original Bund buildings remain intact today, including the Customs House with its clock tower, and the dome-topped Hong Kong and Shanghai Banking Corporation building.**

# HONG KONG

Located on the Pearl River delta in southern China and surrounded by mountains, Hong Kong in its entirety consists of Hong Kong Island, the southern end of the Kowloon Peninsula, and some 230 islands in the South China Sea. Inhabited since the Stone Age, the city began life as a farming and fishing village with a natural harbor, and grew to become a major trading port under the Qing dynasty that ruled China from 1644 to ca. 1912. For a century and a half, from 1842 to

1997, the region was also a British colony. Today, it is one of the most densely populated cities in the world, as well as a major global financial center, with one of the world's busiest ports. It also has more skyscrapers than any other city in the world—in excess of 500 standing 500 feet or taller, and six above a height of 1,000 feet. The tallest, at 1,588 feet, is the International Commerce Centre in Kowloon.

◄ **Victoria Harbour, 1940s,** an aerial view of the harbor, looking across to the Kowloon Peninsula. The harbor had long been a gateway of commerce between the East and the West, becoming integral to the city's growth in the twentieth century.

▼ **Victoria Harbour today,** with the city's tallest skyscraper in the distance. The Hong Kong waterfront has seen considerable development, including the city's second-tallest skyscraper, Two International Finance Centre Tower (1,352 feet).

**STATUE SQUARE** Built on reclaimed land at the turn of the twentieth century, the pedestrianized Statue Square was conceived as a much-needed public space that could also serve as a seat of power during Hong Kong's time as a British colony. It takes its name from the many statues of British monarchs and prominent Hong Kong citizens that once stood here, most notably an impressive bronze statue of Queen Victoria, erected in celebration of her Diamond Jubilee in 1897. Prominent buildings on the square included the city hall, built in 1869, the old Supreme Court Building, which opened in 1912, and the headquarters of the Hong Kong and Shanghai Bank, which has since seen several incarnations.

▶ Statue Square, ca. 1930s. The Neoclassical Supreme Court Building stands to the left of the photograph, with the statue of Queen Victoria taking pride of place at the center of the square. Most of the statues were removed by Japanese occupying forces during World War II. Though many were destroyed, Victoria survived and now stands about two miles away, in Victoria Park.

▲▶ Above: Today, the only remaining statue in the square is that of Sir Thomas Jackson, an early chief of the Hong Kong and Shanghai Bank. Right: The bank's current headquarters, which now dwarf the Supreme Court Building, known today as the Court of Final Appeal.

# TOKYO

Nestling in Tokyo Bay on the island of Honshu, Japan's capital started life as a small fishing village. Originally named Edo, it grew in prominence to become the capital of the Tokugawa shogunate in 1603, with Kyoto as the country's imperial capital. It was not until 1863 that the city was officially renamed Tokyo ("Eastern Capital"). In the first half of the twentieth century, Tokyo was left in ruins by the Great Kantō earthquake of 1923 and then heavily bombed during World

War II. However, rapid postwar reconstruction led to Tokyo becoming the most populous city in the world by 1965, with a population of 20 million. From historic shrines and temples and cherry tree–lined streets, to robot-run hotels, futuristic skyscrapers, and vending machines that sell everything from hamburgers to bananas to umbrellas, Tokyo is like no other city in the world.

◄ **Aerial view of Tokyo, ca. 1945. In May 1945, the United States launched a firebombing raid that laid waste to the city, making more than 1 million homeless. Despite the destruction, the central part of the city was rebuilt within six years.**

▼ **Today, Tokyo is a sprawling metropolis. While the population of the city center is nearly 14 million, the greater metropolitan area now has a population of 37 million.**

**SHIBUYA CROSSING** Tokyo's Shibuya Crossing is a world-famous, much-photographed scramble, or "X," crossing, located in front of the city's Shibuya train station. Originally built in 1973, it is widely regarded as the busiest pedestrian crossing in the world, with as many as 3,000 people crossing each time the traffic lights turn red.

▲ Shibuya, 1950s. Historically, the area had been the site of a castle in which the Shibuya family lived in the eleventh century. With the opening of a train line and station in 1885, it quickly became a commercial and entertainment hub.

▶ Today Shibuya Crossing is a popular tourist destination that has featured in several movies, including *The Fast and the Furious: Tokyo Drift* (2006) and *Lost in Translation* (2003). It even made an appearance in the 2016 Summer Olympics closing ceremony.

# SYDNEY

Set on the Pacific Ocean in New South Wales and lined with more than a hundred beaches, Sydney is known as the Emerald City. Before colonization by the British in 1788, the land on which the city sits had been inhabited for tens of thousands of years by the first peoples of the country and is the territory of the Gadigal people. Surrounded by national parks with Ku-ring-gai Chase National Park to the north, the Royal National Park to the south, and the Blue Mountains to the west, Sydney sits on one of the world's largest natural harbors, site of two architectural masterpieces, the Sydney Opera House and the Sydney Harbour Bridge, known affectionately by locals as the "Coathanger."

◀◀ Sydney Harbour, also known as Port Jackson, 1895. The bridge was built to connect the city, seen in the foreground here, to its northern suburbs across the water.

◀ The bridge under construction, 1930. Work began with the building of the north and south approach ways, with two concrete piers erected on each side of the harbor to support the bridge's arch. On completion, it was one of the longest steel bridges in the world, spanning an estimated 1,650 feet.

▼ Sydney Harbour today. Having first opened in 1932, the bridge carries eight traffic lanes, railway tracks, a bike path, and a pedestrian walkway. A set of stairs leads to the center of the arch.

**SYDNEY OPERA HOUSE** As one of the best-known and most iconic buildings in the world, the Sydney Opera House is the jewel in this city's crown. Designed by Danish architect Jørn Utzon, this modern Expressionist building was created using a number of precast concrete shells, or "sails," that sit upon a huge podium and are covered in tiny white and cream chevron-patterned tiles.

▼ Sydney's Circular Quay, 1932, showing the building site for the Sydney Opera House on Bennelong Point, sitting directly in front of the Royal Botanic Garden.

◄ The Sydney Opera House under construction. More than 233 designs had been submitted for its design as part of an international competition. The Opera House was officially opened by Queen Elizabeth II in 1973.

◀ Left: The Sydney Opera House, 2022. Initially, construction was expected to take four years, but it ended up taking fourteen years and involved more than 10,000 construction workers, with work commencing in 1959.

▼ Below: Aerial view of present-day Sydney Harbour, with the towers of the central business district rising between the Sydney Opera House and the Sydney Harbour Bridge.

# INDEX

# PICTURE CREDITS

The publisher would like to thank the following for the permission to reproduce copyrighted material.

**Alamy:** 4k-Clips: 88 (right), 89 (right); Agencja Fotograficzna Caro: 116 (right); Bailey-Cooper Photography: 77; Louis Berk: 98 (top right), 98 (bottom right); ClassicStock: 50; colaimages: 112 (top); Ian Dagnall: 140 (right); dpa picture alliance: 7 (left), 116 (left), 118 (left), 119 (top); Everett Collection Historical: 142; eye35.pix: 143; FLHC 10: 154 (bottom); Gado Images: 106 (bottom left); GRANGER - Historical Picture Archive: 113 (left, top and bottom); Heritage Image Partnership Ltd: 22, 38, 40; History and Art Collection: 34 (top), 35 (top right); INTERFOTO: 120 (top); Lebrecht Music & Arts: 124 (left); 125 (left); Lucky-photographer: 39; 50; MARKA: 122, 128, 130; Niday Picture Library: 76; Pictorial Press Ltd: 10; The Print Collector: 152; David Richards: 99 (center), 99 (bottom right); robertharding: 135, 139; Vladyslav Siaber: 131; State Archives of Florida/Florida Memory: 88 (left), 89 (left); Underwood Archives: 20 (top); Joe Vella: 110.

**City of Vancouver Archives:** Stuart Thomson: 32 (top).

**Dreamstime:** © Alexey Fedorenko: 115; Saiko3p: 93 (bottom).

**Flickr:** Seattle Municipal Archives: 28.

**Get Archive:** Maison Bonfils (Beirut, Lebanon), photographer: 132.

**Getty:** AaronP/Bauer-Griffin: 13; Archive Photos/Stringer 62; Arterra: 55; ASMR: 149; Scott E Barbour: 136 (right); Bettmann: 12, 19 (top), 20 (bottom), 26, 46 (left), 47 (top), 90, 92 (top), 94 (top left), 144; Bloomberg: 141 (bottom); Alex Bowie: 140 (left); brandstaetter images: 126 (top right); Jon Brenneis: 42 (bottom); Central Press/Stringer: 99 (left), 99 (top right); Chicago History Museum: 44; george clerk: 97; Culture Club: 114, 126 (bottom left), 127 (right); Daily Herald Archive: 146; Eloi_Omella: 75;  PATRICK T. FALLON: 59; Fotosearch/Stringer: 70 (top), 71 (left); fotoVoyager: 19 (bottom); FPG: 33 (top right); General Photographic Agency/Stringer: 138; H. Armstrong

Roberts/ClassicStock: 54, 64; Helifilms Australia: 52; Heritage Images: 100 (bottom), 102; H.F. Davis/Stringer: 98 (top left), 98 bottom left); Hulton Archive: 153 (top); Hulton Deutsch: 117 (top); John Parrot/Stocktrek Images: 74; Paul Kaye: 96, 158–159; Keystone-France: 24; Keystone/Stringer: 42 (top);  Larry Lee Photography: 72 (right); Frederic Lewis: 86 (right), 87 bottom); Library of Congress: 2 (left), 8, 78 (left), 79 (top); London Stereoscopic Company: 100 (top left); Manjurul Haque/EyeEm: 34 (bottom); @ Didier Marti: 147; Michel Suesse/EyeEm 69 (right); Mlenny: 46 (right), 47 (bottom); James D. Morgan: 155 (bottom); F J Mortimer: 100 (top right); The New York Historical Society: 80 (top left); nicolamargaret: 91;  Orlando/Stringer: 150; Pictorial Parade: 84; Pictorial Parade/Stringer: 154 (top); Popperfoto: 141 (top); RICOWde: 117 (bottom); Joel Rogers: 27; Salvatore Liguigli/Eyeem: 70 (bottom); Alexander Spatari: 81; Gabriel Sperandio: 95; Spotmatik: 45; Justin Sullivan: 18; Mario Tarna: 58; temmuzcan: 35 (bottom); ullstein bild: 120 (bottom); Universal History Archive: 72 (left), 80 (bottom left), 80 (right); University of Southern California: 14 (left), 15 (top); Barry Winiker: 123; zhuyufang: 145.

**House Divided:** Brady-Handy Collection, Library of Congress Prints and Photographs Division: 70 (center).

**iStock:** Chris LaBasco: 23; KathrynHatashitaLee: 33 (bottom right); milehightraveler: 133; Alena_Saz: 25; simonkr: 15 (bottom); tifonimages: 65; Art Wager: 53.

**Shutterstock:** Andrey Bayda: 11; beboy: 107 (top); Blue Planet Studio: 112 (bottom); Canadastock: 21; Nejdet Duzen: 49 (top); EB Adventure Photography: 37; Everett Collection: 16, 56 (left), 57 (top), 66; Igor Golovniov: 104; Mario Hagen: 29; Kamira: 86 (left), 87 (top); Punyaphat Larpsomboon: 147 (left);Viacheslav Lopatin: 106 (bottom right); Mickis-Fotowelt: 121; Trong Nguyen: 61; Sean Pavone: 51; Photocarioca: 94 (top right); photosounds: 63; Enrico Della Pietra: 56 (right), 57 (bottom); Stefan Rotter: 129; Loic Salan: 107 (bottom); Sandor Szmutko: 101; travelview: 41; TTstudio: 126 (bottom right), 127 (left); Underwood Archives/UIG/Shutterstock: 108 (bottom); Vlas Telino studio: 111; Taras Vyshnya: 153 (bottom); Ken Wolter: 14 (right), 15 (center); Andrew Zarivny: 17.

**Unsplash:** Josue Aguazia: 73 right; Ahmed Aldaie: 137; Anthony DELANOIX: 109; Clément Dellandrea: 82 (left), 83 (bottom); Andy Feliciotti: 9; Shawn Henley: 85; Fas Khan: 103; Rodrigo Kugnharski: 105; Bastian Pudill: 7 (right), 118 (right), 119 (bottom); Mathew Schwartz: 156–157; Nico Smit: 155 (top); Ryan Stone 69 (left); Cris Tagupa: 2 (right), 78 (right), 79 (bottom); Philipp Torres: 124 (right), 125 (right); Timo Volz: 151; Unseen Histories: 68 (right); zhan zhang: 43.

**Wikimedia Commons:** 108 (top, left to right); 1851 photo from collection of Micaela Almonester via Photographer in employ of Micaela Almonester, 1851: 60; Aheilner: 136 (left); Author unknown. From the collection of Matthews, James Skitt, Major (1878¬–1970): 35 (top left); Édouard Baldus (1813–1889): 106 (top); BiblioArchives/LibraryArchives from Canada: 33 (top left); Mathew Benjamin Brady – Library of Congress Prints and Photographs Division. Brady-Handy Photograph Collection: 68 (left); Brooklyn Museum @ Flickr Commons: 82 (right), 83 (top); FJC: 48; David G. Gordon: 31; Gobierno de la Ciudad Autónoma de Buenos Aires: 92 (bottom); Andreas Groll/Wien Museum: 126 (top left); Carol M. Highsmith – Library of Congress's Prints and Photographs Division 67; IMS Collection: 94 (bottom); Catalin Manolescu: 113 (right, top and bottom); MJ: 32 (bottom); MRDXII: 33 (bottom left); William McFarlane Notman/McCord Stewart Museum: 30; OSU Special Collections & Archives : Commons: 93 (top); Prasanaik: 134; Harold G Prenter, Pacific Survey Corporation, Vancouver: 36; TonyTheTiger: 49 (bottom); US Army Signal Corps: 148; The U.S. National Archives: 73 (left).

While every effort has been made to credit photographers, The Bright Press would like to apologize should there have been any omissions or errors, and would be pleased to make the appropriate correction for future editions of the book.